Art&lots of dots Gallery
invites you to **exhibit works of art**
you and your friends make in
this room created especially for you

DISCARD

Art&lots *of dots*
Basic concepts of art

Texts
Ginett Alarcón F. and Marisa Mena

Illustrations
Yonel Hernández

Research
Glenda Dorta

Translation
Lisa Blackmore

Art&lots *of dots* was produced
by Editemos.
A print run of 2000 was made
at Panamericana Formas e Impresos, S.A.,
Bogotá, Colombia, in the month of May 2011.

Typographic characters from the Glypha
and Bodoni Lt family were used.
It was printed on offset 115 and 150 g paper
and the cover on Cote C2S 300 g card.

Printed in Colombia – *Impreso en Colombia*
Legal Deposit lf25220107003662
ISBN 978-980-739-00-9

©Editemos, 2011
©Yonel Hernández, 2011
©The artists and their inheritors, 2011

The partial or total reproduction of this book
is prohibited. All rights reserved.

www.editemos.com
info@editemos.com

Information, comments.
Tell us how do you imagine your own book of art:
arteypunto@editemos.com

Art&lots of dots

Basic concepts of art

Illustrations *Yonel Hernández*

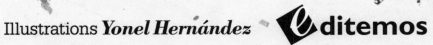

Dots

Are a vital element in art. They are created when we make contact with a surface (paper, canvas, wood or metal) using a pencil, a paintbrush or another instrument. When we draw a **dot**, it usually represents a small, **round** ●, but it can also be **square** ■, **rectangular** ▬, **triangular** ▲, or just a **mark** ⬤.

Their size also varies. The image on the television screen is made up of **rectangular dots but our eyes don't see them.**

We can make shapes by creating groups of dots without drawing lines.
For example, **pointillism** is a painting technique that was created in France at the end of the 19th century. It uses different **colored dots** that produce a clear image when we look at them from a distance.

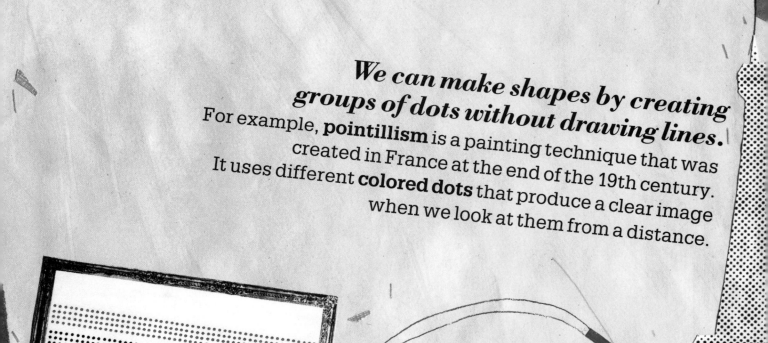

Lines

Are a continual succession of dots.

In drawings we use **straight lines** (horizontal, vertical, oblique),

curved lines, whose dots change direction,

or **mixed lines**, which are made when we mix straight and curved lines.

We can make a work of art by just using lines.

Lines can define **geometric** ◯ or **figurative** , shapes, **space** ▢,

volume ● and **mo** ⟶ **vement**

Lines can also trigger emotions.

Texture

Is what the surface of objects is like.
Or, in other words, it is their external appearance.

If we compare different materials (stone, fabric, marble, metal, glass or paper), we will find that some are **rough** and others are **smooth**, they have different textures.

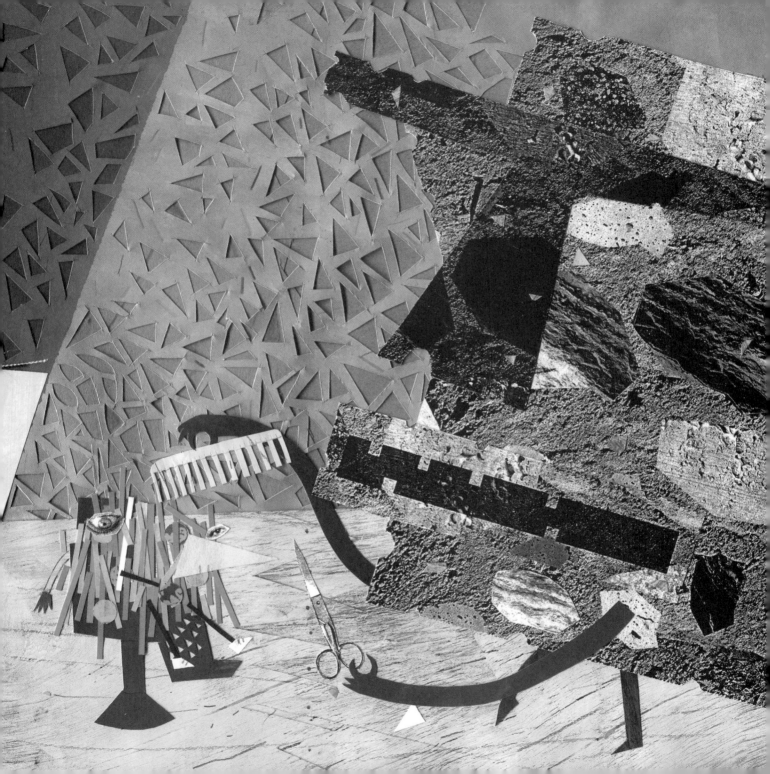

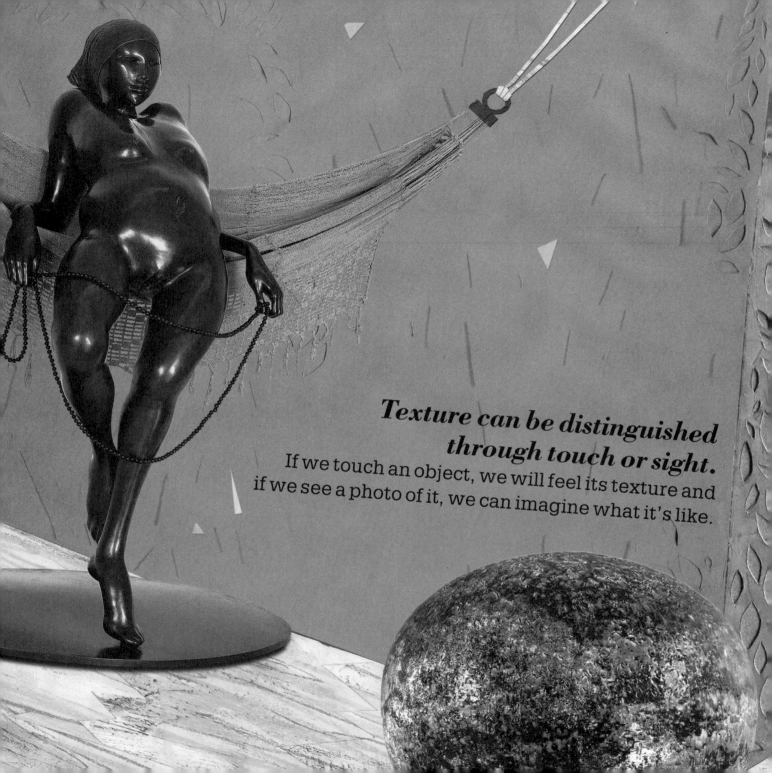

Texture can be distinguished through touch or sight.
If we touch an object, we will feel its texture and if we see a photo of it, we can imagine what it's like.

Tonal values

Are the maximum lightness or darkness of a color.

Greys are the intermediate values between black and white.

In a dark room we find it difficult to make out the objects around us, because light allows us to see their shapes and colors.

Luminosity is the amount of light reflected by the surface of matter.

When we paint, white has the most **luminosity** and black means there is no **luminosity**.

The **silhouette** technique allows us to gradually distribute **light** and **shadow** to show the volume of objects.

Color

Is the visual impression caused when light impacts on matter.

To paint we need **primary colors** , **secondary colors** produced by mixing primary colors, or **tertiary colors** , made by mixing one secondary and one primary color.

The differences that we can see between the same color are caused by the following qualities:

Tint is the color itself.

Tonal value is the amount of light in that color.

Saturation is the intensity or purity of a color. If we add black, white or a complementary color, the color will lose its purity.

If when two colors are mixed together using certain proportions they make a neutral color, these two colors are **complementary** ● + ● = ●

Dots

Elsa Morales
Ella y la luna
2000
Acrylic on canvas
59.7 x 50 cm
FMN collection,
Museo Arturo Michelena
Photo Archive
Museo Arturo Michelena

JJ Moros
Sideros
1994
Soldered and polished iron
131 of diameter x 20,5 cm
Empresas Polar collection
Photo Archive JJ Moros

Mario Abreu
Selva amazónica
1956
Oil on canvas
89.5 x 179.5 cm
FMN collection, Galería de Arte Nacional
Photo Archive Cinap

Jesús Soto
Untitled (Étude pour une série)
1952-1953
Paint on wood
102 x 102 x 6 cm
Museo de Arte Moderno
Jesús Soto collection
Photo Luis Brito and Ramón Lepage

Lines

Manasés
Sirena negra
1981
Acrylic on canvas
150 x 100 cm
FMN collection,
Galería de Arte Nacional
Photo Archive Cinap

Jesús Guerrero
Cancha
2001
Acrylic and charcoal
on waxed canvas
240 x 240 cm
Artist's collection
Photo Eduardo Paparoni

Gego
Partiendo de un rectángulo II
1958
Bent, screwed and
enamelled aluminium strip
32 x 36 x 37 cm
Privada Allegro Foundation collection
Photo Luis Becerra

Texture

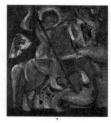

Seka
P-2
Undated
Pottery, earthenware,
oxides and enamels
58 x 45 cm of diameter
FMN collection,
Museo de Arte Contemporáneo
Photo Morella Muñoz-Tébar

Alirio Palacios
San Jorge
1997
Engraved sheet of wood
195 x 260 cm
Artist's collection
Photo Renato Donzelli

Cornelis Zitman
L'inconnue (Mujer en hamaca)
1972
Patinized bronze,
woven vegetable fibre and seeds
184 x 251 x 125 cm
FMN collection, Galería de Arte Nacional
Photo Archive Cinap

Tonal value

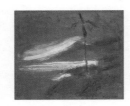

Bárbaro Rivas
Autorretrato
1964
Industrial enamel
on paper maché
59.5 x 43 cm
FMN collection,
Galería de Arte Nacional
Photo Archive Cinap

Armando Reverón
Cocotero
Circa 1944
Tempera and sand
on canvas
50.3 x 58.3 cm
FMN collection,
Galería de Arte Nacional
Photo Archive Cinap

Arturo Michelena
El niño enfermo
1886
Oil on canvas
80.4 x 85 cm
FMN collection,
Galería de Arte Nacional
Photo Archive Cinap

Color

Carlos Cruz-Diez
Color aditivo,
Serie junio 10ECD
2003
Cromolithography on
canvas
(original of an edition of 3)
80 x 80 cm
Artist's collection
Photo Atelier Cruz-Diez

Mercedes Pardo
Composición
1959
Oil on canvas
100 x 150 cm
FMN collection,
Galería de Arte Nacional
Photo Archive Cinap

Alejandro Otero
Coloritmo N.º 4
1956
Duco on wood
186.1 x 46 x 3.2 cm
Mercantil collection
Photo Archive Mercantil

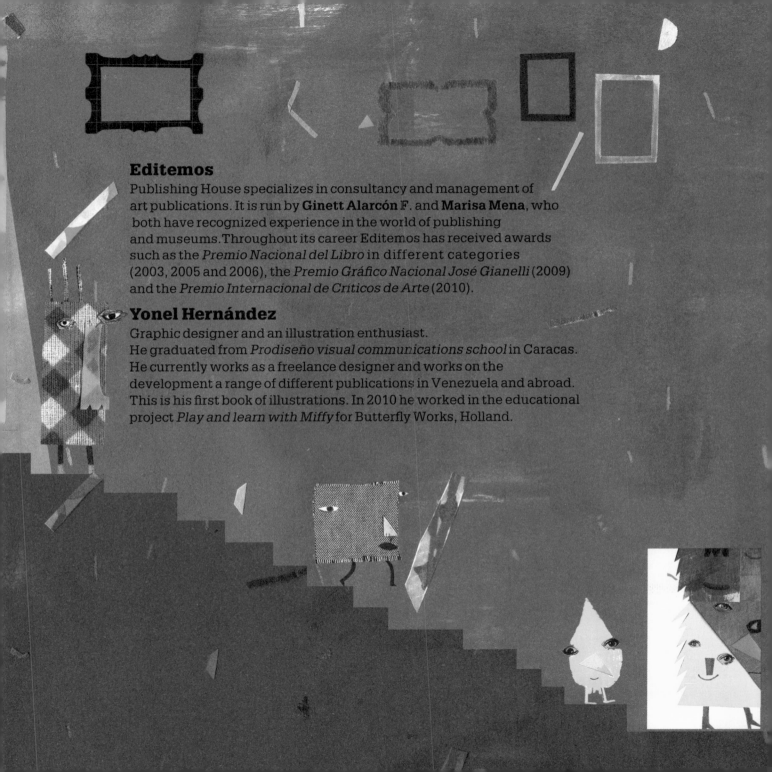

Editemos

Publishing House specializes in consultancy and management of art publications. It is run by **Ginett Alarcón** F. and **Marisa Mena**, who both have recognized experience in the world of publishing and museums. Throughout its career Editemos has received awards such as the *Premio Nacional del Libro* in different categories (2003, 2005 and 2006), the *Premio Gráfico Nacional José Gianelli* (2009) and the *Premio Internacional de Criticos de Arte* (2010).

Yonel Hernández

Graphic designer and an illustration enthusiast.
He graduated from *Prodiseño visual communications school* in Caracas. He currently works as a freelance designer and works on the development a range of different publications in Venezuela and abroad. This is his first book of illustrations. In 2010 he worked in the educational project *Play and learn with Miffy* for Butterfly Works, Holland.